# Cool is the Guitar

The Easy to Learn for Kids Guitar Course

Jon P Fox

Copyright © 2014 Jon P Fox

All rights reserved.

ISBN-13: 9781500472542
ISBN-10: 1500472549

# Copyright Information

*Copyright: Published in the United States by Jon P Fox / © Jon P Fox 2014*

*All rights reserved. No part of this publication may be reproduced, stored in retrieval system, copied in any form or by any means, electronic, mechanical, photocopying, recording or otherwise transmitted without written permission from the publisher. Please do not participate in or encourage piracy of this material in any way. You must not circulate this book in any format. Jon P Fox does not control or direct users' actions and is not responsible for the information or content shared, harm and/or actions of the book readers.*

*In accordance with the U.S. Copyright Act of 1976, the scanning, uploading and electronic sharing of any part of this book without the permission of the publisher constitutes unlawful piracy and theft of the author's intellectual property. If you would like to use material from the book (other than just simply for reviewing the book), prior permission must be obtained by contacting the author at jonpf239@gmail.com*

*Thank you for your support of the author's rights.*

# DEDICATION

I want to thank My Mother who has passed on in September of 2013, God Bless Her Soul, for all the encouragement she gave me and how she stood behind me as I was growing up throughout school and learning to play guitar. Mom bought me my first guitar from a respected band member that no longer used the old guitar. But I just loved it. The guitar was a Guild hollow body electric guitar that was very cool. I wish I still had it today.

And to my Dad who is a musician himself and always had a guitar around the house as I was growing up. He encouraged me to be in the band and music class at school and always stood behind me as I was growing up. He bought me my first alto saxophone as well as showed me my first lesson on the guitar. Although I ended up using a beginner book to teach me he showed me what it is like to make sounds and play strings on a guitar. Dad took me to the symphony concerts when I was only a little boy and always backed my interests in music. Thank You to Mom and Dad!

To Mr. Moore, Mr. Dorjaph, and Mr. Flanagan all of which were band and music teachers of mine during elementary, Jr. High and High School. Thanks guys for helping me to understand the world of music and how to do something with it. Oh and thank you for giving me the good grades. ☺

# CONTENTS

# Introduction

As a very young child I have seen the guitar in the hands of many people, both right in front of me and on the TV or Stage. I always thought that the guitar was so cool. Of course my Father had a couple of guitars right there in our home. Sometimes Dad would leave the guitar leaning in a corner and I would take it and strum the strings. I would think: 'This is neat, the way these strings make sounds like that!'

But when I remembered my Dad playing it, he made it sound much better and we all used to sing along when he would play. But I couldn't understand how he could use his fingers to hold the strings and make the music come out of it. I would put my fingers on it and try but it wouldn't work, so I would put it down and just wonder how people could take their fingers and make that guitar sound so neat.

Then one day after seeing the guitar leaning in the corner again, I decided that I really wanted to learn how to make it sound neat like other people do no matter how long it will take me. I had a moment that I was determined to learn how to use my fingers and make that guitar sound cool. But I needed help! So I asked my Mom and Dad to get me some lessons. Mom and Dad told me that they will buy me a book and Dad said after I finish the book he will give me lessons from there.

So I thought of it like the same as in school, like the lessons we learn from our school book with the teacher, only this lesson will be done with a book at home. So then it started. My Mom got me a beginners guitar book and I started at page one. I worked from that book until I could do what it was talking about. It took me a lot of trying day after day but soon I could do it. Yeah! I could make the strings sound like music, not as well as Dad but I could do it now! Cool is the guitar.

In this book you will learn just as I did, a little at a time and the fastest and easiest way to possibly learn to make music using a guitar. I will turn back time, and I will remember the frustration I experienced and try and make it so simple that all it will take is just read, do, and do again. With a little practice you will make music. Don't care how well someone else can play a guitar; you just do it a little at a time. You have your whole life ahead of you to show them! ☺

# 1 GENERAL GUITAR INFORMATION

Hopefully as you are reading this book you now have a guitar! I know you are more than excited to play your favorite songs with that guitar.

But did you know that even people who lived hundreds of years ago also played guitars? That is because guitars first existed way back in 1400's in Spain. But even though guitars were first played in 1400's, people already started making guitar-like instruments even before that. In theory, it was in 1100's that the first guitar-like instrument was

created and played. That was in Europe.

As we all know, the guitars that we use these days have six strings. And we call them "six string guitars". But when guitars were first used before, there were three sets of double strings and then one single string. Also, early guitars used to be made with the use of animal guts. It was only in the year 1946 when guitar makers decided to use nylon for the guitars' strings. Over time the Spanish guitar developed to use nylon strings as the bottom three because of the way that they sounded.

Many Spanish guitarists prefer the nylon sound over steel strings, on the bottom three. (Myth Buster: The nylon strings are not used on a guitar to make it easy for a beginner to learn to play!)

Andres Segovia, who lived until the year 1987, is considered by many to be the most popular classical guitarist. He used to play lots of classical music with the use of his guitar. Aside from Andres Segovia, Leo Fender and Les Paul are also big names in the subject of guitars and they became part of a huge industry. Fender and Paul were the ones who developed the very first solid body electric guitars in 1940's.

Franz Schubert was also a famous composer who played the guitar. Schubert used to compose music with the use of his guitar. He did his work in the early 1800's and of course people loved Franz Schubert's music which was so popular, and many still do today.

Another popular name in the guitar industry is Benjamin Franklin. Yes, he is one of the Founding Fathers of the United States and was a great inventor, whom which contributed much to society. But he also played the guitar.

I hope this information helps you to see that there are many people who enjoy playing the guitar, both a long long time ago and today! That is because this instrument is very versatile and fun to play. So since you have become interested in playing as well, let's go ahead and begin to learn. Now is a great time for you to learn the easiest way to get used to, and begin playing the guitar!

# 2 STRINGED INSTRUMENTS

The world is full of stringed instruments actually. The guitar is not alone in the stringed instrument family. There are the ukulele, violin, harp, cello, banjo, viola, and many more. Look at the picture below to see what these instruments look like.

# THE STRING FAMILY

Also in the string family there are some instruments that do not have a neck such as: the piano, and the harp. The acoustic piano is among the very oldest string instrument known to man. The strings in this instrument are located inside the big box which is built around the keyboard, and comes in many

different sizes.

But perhaps the most common and popular instrument among all these string instruments is the guitar. The guitar seems to be the most popular string instrument and is most often used to be played by itself. Unlike some of the instruments in the picture above which are used mostly in symphonic bands. But they all come from the same family.

A guitar is basically a stringed instrument that makes sound just by passing your fingers across its six strings. I bet you have tried that already. You can either pluck the strings or strum them, depending on what you want the sound to be like.

Have you already seen different guitars? Some of them do not look like your guitar, right? There are some guitars that are not like the others. That is because guitars have several different types: There are acoustic guitars which are hollow, electric guitars which are solid, electric guitars that are hollow, and there are left handed guitars as well as steel guitars and what's known as a do-bro. The Do-bro was developed in the 1950's by the Dopĕra Brothers.

Since these guitars are all different, they also produce different types of sounds, (except the left handed ones). They produce different sounds because naturally they are made different. If you have an acoustic guitar the sound comes from the hollow part. If you have a solid body guitar, or electric guitar, the sound will be artificial.

That means you will have to plug it into an amplifier so that the pickups can send the sound that comes from the strings to that amplifier. Sometimes a musician wants to have the sound of the hollow body guitar on purpose, even if they have both kinds of guitars. In this book, we will focus more on playing an acoustic guitar since this is an instrument that does not need any other components just to play it and be able to hear it.  Now, let us take a look into the different parts of an acoustic guitar.

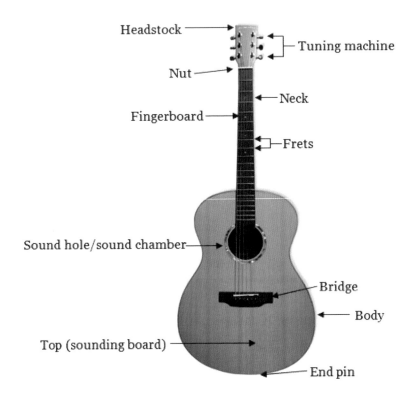

1. **Body**. That part of the guitar which is shaped like the number eight is called the body.  The body is purposely built hollow to create a sound acoustic.  Just like if you place your phone in a bowl with the music player on. So now when you pluck or strum the strings you can hear the sound very well.

2. **Bridge**. Do you see a plate on the guitar that holds all the strings together? That is what is known as the bridge.  Many guitars are made with adjustable bridges that can be adjusted up or down. Yours may be a fixed bridge however.  The bridge holds the strings in place so that the tuning keys can tighten the strings.  It also connects the strings to the guitar's body.

3. **End Pin**. The end pin can also be called a peg; is the plastic or metal post at the bottom of your guitar. Its purpose is to hook the shoulder strap, so that it will be easier for you to hold the guitar while standing up. The end pin has a partner located at the top of the "guitar body" attached to the back of the neck. Note: You may come across acoustic guitars that don't have these pegs; in that case you will have to play using a seat. You can have a technician install strap pegs as well. I don't recommend tying a string around the guitar because that will cause the neck to slightly move and it will play out of tune.

4. **Fingerboard**. The fingerboard is also called the fret board and is that top layer of wood that is fastened on the face of the guitar's neck. It is made from a harder wood type than the rest of the neck and sometimes will have Perl inlays (Nifty little jewels that are pressed into the wood and keep it from wearing down from long-time use). The fingerboard is where you place your fingers so that you will be able to produce notes and chords.

5. **Frets**. The frets are the little metal strips that are pressed into the wood of the fingerboard. Most guitars have 20 frets. When you press a string down onto the fret, it shortens the length of the string. That causes the string to vibrate shorter and makes a higher sound, so that there will be different pitches produced. That is why the pitch produced when you place your fingers on the first fret is different from the pitch produced when you place your fingers on the second fret, or third fret, and so on.

6. **Headstock**. The headstock is the end part of the guitar's neck. This is where the tuning keys are located. Also, many times guitar manufacturers place their logos on the headstock so you can look there to see what kind of guitar you have, or who made it.

7. **Neck**. The neck is that long piece of wood that is connected to the body of your guitar. The neck and headstock are all one piece of wood. The neck is also what has that fingerboard that is made out of harder wood, attached to it for its face. One more thing that the neck has is

the calibrating rod or a support rod for some guitars, going through the center of it which keeps the guitar neck from warping.

8. **Nut**. As you will see on your guitar, there is a line between the headstock and the neck. That is known as the guitar's nut. It was typically made from ivory but not all guitars. The purpose of the nut is to position each string properly and prevent the strings from vibrating past the neck, as well as keeping the strings up off the fingerboard. If the strings touch the fingerboard frets they will rattle and it won't be able to sound right. So the nut has to mark the point as to where the vibrating area of the string will end, and keep the strings up above the metal frets.

9. **Strings**. I am certain you know what the strings are! There are usually six strings on a guitar. When you strum or pluck these strings, you will be able to produce notes and chords. The top four strings on your acoustic guitar will be fatter than the rest because they are nickel wound. (That means they are wound by a machine where it wraps a string around another string making the two strings one big string) The bottom three are known as plain strings and sometimes the guitar owner will install those bottom three strings using nylon strings instead of plain steel ones for the unique sound of nylon.

10. **Top**. Almost no need to even note this part but the top is simply the top part of the body where you could tap on it along the way while playing to make a percussion or a drumming sound; many have adapted this style when playing their guitar.

11. **Tuning machines**. A tuning machine is the entire housing from which the tuning key sticks out. When you turn the tuning key the little gear inside moves the stud with the little hole that has the string running through it. That key will make the string tight or loose and this is what changes the pitch from lower to higher. (Or the other way around) The tighter the strings are, the higher the pitch will be. The looser the strings are, the lower the pitch will be, and it is the tuning machines that get the job done. Of course these aren't really actual

machines because they are not self powered...YET! ☺

**So that is the explanation of the parts of the acoustic guitar.** You probably won't care much about these identifying parts and their definitions all that much until you begin to talk guitars to your friends and the folks down at the music store. But just know that you can always reference this book if you need to tell someone about a certain part of your guitar.

You want to be sure not to leave your guitar where it can fall over and break the headstock or a tuning key. Also don't take all the strings off and then let the guitar sit without strings for days, because you are waiting for a new set to come in the mail. This will cause the neck to warp a little and if your guitar cannot be re-calibrated then you won't be able to tune the guitar well with the warped neck ever again. (And Mom won't be too happy either.☹)

So it is things like that to be aware of and just take care of your guitar very well. Always place it back into the case and close the case clips when you finish playing it.

# 3 LEARNING TO HOLD THE GUITAR

Now that we have already talked about the different parts of a guitar, let's go ahead and discuss how to properly hold the guitar. The typical way of holding the guitar is having your left hand holding the neck while the right hand is strumming or plucking the strings. But there are some who hold the guitar the other way around. They have their right hand hold the guitar's neck while their left hand plucks or strums the strings. A left handed guitarist has to purchase a guitar made just for him or her.

Your chair or seat should be the right one for your height. Do not sit on a chair that is too low for you. That will make your knees bend higher, which will make holding the guitar difficult for you. You should not sit on a seat that is too high for you also. Your legs will be too stretched, and they will not be able to support your guitar. Therefore, you need to make sure that you are sitting on a seat that is just right for your height.

When holding the guitar to play it, use a strap at all times if you can. Not all guitars will have strap pegs however, if this is the case, you need to make sure that your knees will be able to support your guitar well. You will place the body of your guitar on your thighs or knees as you play, so make sure that your knees can raise your guitar high enough that it is still easy to play.

Up to this point I have not mentioned the pick yet. I am sure you have seen guitar picks at one time or another but if not. The guitar pick is that flat, usually triangular cool looking little piece of plastic or nylon. They are used to pick or pluck, and strum the strings instead of using fingers only. There will be times to go with a pick and times to do what guitarists call "fingerpick'. (The terms "Finger picking" comes from the use of these little plastic picks that can clip onto your fingers, but guitarists also call it 'finger picking' when they play the guitar without any pick at all.) If you got yourself a pick when you obtained your guitar then let's use it. Neither a strap nor a pick are absolutely necessary however, and some believe that you should practice playing the guitar without either one, so that you are not dependent upon additives just to be able to play.

The most important thing that you have to consider when holding your guitar is whether you feel comfortable enough holding it. Also, you have to make sure that you can properly place your fingers on the guitar's frets. This took me a long time to get used to so I want you to start out the right way the first time. See the picture 'Figure 1'.

Notice how the thumb is kept below the top of the neck, somewhere around the middle of the back of that guitar neck. The reason for this is to learn to start holding your thumb low behind the neck as you begin to learn to play the guitar. As you get better you will find that it was much easier to hold down the strings when your thumb is down lower behind the neck. It makes your hand work more like a sort of vise clamp and you can hold the strings down without developing a hand cramp.

There are many guitarists in the world that let their thumb go high on the back of the neck but they went through a lot of pain getting used to that unless of course they were just double jointed or have very large hands. None-the-less; many people break general beginner rules and go with whatever comes natural to them, but they also learn the hard way and this book is all about teaching how to play this instrument the easiest way possible.

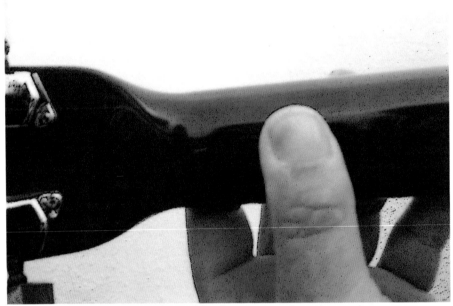

Figure 1: Properly positioning the hand on the neck.

Figure 1 above is showing the **starting point** to place your hand when playing the guitar. It is particularly showing where the thumb should be in general. The thumb will however move around as you work the strings and play chords. Learning the proper position right from the start will save you from developing in an awkward way that will cause your hand to hurt. Plus doing it wrong could cause you to not grow and play as the very best that you could. (Full Potential) ☺

# 4 HOW TO TUNE MY GUITAR

Before we play a song with your guitar, it will be a good idea to make sure that your guitar is properly tuned. If it is not tuned, then when you play a chord or song, it will not sound right. Meaning the sound will be incorrect and will be just noise instead of music. No matter how well you hold the strings onto the frets and how well you can do the chords (we will talk about chords later in this book); your song will still be out of tune if your guitar is out of tune.

So now, we will talk about how you should tune your guitar. Do not worry if this does not come easy for you. It is still your first time to do this, after all. This may seem to be a little bit complicated at first, but after you do this a few times, you will then be able to do it very well. (Just like when you get better on your video game!)

When you are tuning your guitar, knowing the names of each string will be first. Take a look at 'figure 2':

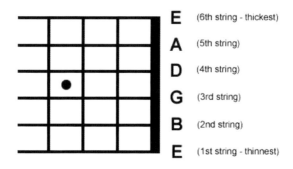

Figure 2: Names of the Strings.

All musical instruments are created in a certain key. Talking about musical key signatures is a subject that is a little more advanced than the training in this book, but I want you to start out by at least knowing that the your six string acoustic guitar was created in the key of 'E'. That means its lowest note is E. Some people change the key that their guitar is in on purpose by tuning it to a different key, but you would have to re-learn all chords and notes for that key. (See how some artist's are?) We won't do that though. We will tune the guitar in the key that the instrument was created to be in which is 'E'

Look at the strings of your guitar. You can see six strings, right? And of course they are not the same, actually each string has is a different thickness.

And because of this, each string produces a different sound as compared to the others, they are designed to be different from one another but work together.

The thickest of all the strings on your guitar is called the low E-string. (This is the key signature that the guitar is created in). It is called 'low E' because it is the E note when tuned right, and it is the lowest E note on the guitar. Try plucking the low E-string, then pluck the string next to it, the low E-string sounds lower in pitch, right?

After the low E-string, or the ones just below it, you have the A-string, then the D-string, the G-string, and then the B-string. The last string is the thinnest one. It is named the high E-string. Try not to get confused with the picture shown above. Yes, there are two E-strings. The only difference between them is that the low E-String is the thickest string, while the High E-String is the thinnest string, but when plucked they both are the E note. (The low E and the high E)

When tuning, you need to set the low E to the E note. When you got your guitar it probably came with the note set to E. If not you will need the folks at the music store help you with that. Once you have the thickest string set to the E note, you just have to press down that string on the fifth fret and pluck it. To know which fret is the fifth fret, just count from the very first fret (from the headstock). Now that you have your finger on the E string at the fifth fret, pluck the string and listen to the pitch. That is the pitch the A string needs to be. When you set the A string to that pitch it will be the 'A note'. Let us say that you are tuning the D-string, just hold the D-string on the fifth fret, and then pluck the string. (That string only; not the others).

Hold each string one at a time at the fifth fret. Pluck the string while holding the fifth fret and then pluck the string below the one you are holding. If the one below does not sound the same as the one you are holding on the fifth fret, then turn the tuning key either toward you or away from you to make the string sound the same as the one you are holding down. You will do this for each string **except the G string**. You will hold down the **G string on the fourth fret, but only the G string.** Once you hold down the G string on the fourth fret, go ahead and pluck it and then listen to it; now pluck the B string and listen to it.

Does the B string sound the same as the G string does with you holding it at the fourth fret? If not, then turn its tuning key until it sounds the same. But when you get to the next one you will go back to holding down the string on the fifth fret again.

If they do not sound the same, then your guitar is out of tune. Then you just follow what is written above until each string has been set right. Just adjust the string's keys at the tuning machine. Turn the tuning machine once lightly, and listen to how it sounds and see if you need to tune higher or lower to the string.

**Note:**

Maybe someone in your family or yourself can get a little help to set the tuning, with a download of tuning software. If so here is one that is free to download: http://www.nch.com.au/tuner/ If that software is not there anymore, just do a search for "Download Free Guitar Tuner" on the Internet.

You should always learn to tune by ear though. Just follow the steps explained in this book, get help with this section because it is important that you learn how to tune your guitar and you will know how to tune any guitar at any time for life.

If you keep on adjusting the tuning machines, there will be a possibility that your string will break. That will happen if you turn the tuning machine too tight. There will also be a problem if you turn it too loose. Your string will loosen, and it will not sound right at all.

# 5 PLAYING SINGLE NOTES

In this chapter we will go into how to play just single notes on the guitar. This is a great way to learn how to hold down strings and make sounds one note at a time. When I was learning, the instructions basically only taught me chords. But what if I wanted to learn how to play lead guitar? If all we ever learn are the chords then that could be all we ever do with a guitar, play chords.

But that would be a tragedy. The world needs both lead guitarists and rhythm guitarists. Now some things about learning to play a guitar are going to prove to be too advanced for this book. However I am certain that you can pick up on what I will teach you here in this chapter.

In order to play single notes we will go back to what we were doing when we were tuning the guitar. Yeck! You might be saying at this point but don't worry, I am not talking about doing more tuning but that when you were tuning that guitar you were playing single notes. The notes were the main notes of the strings. They were E, A, D, G, B, and E. Now instead of just playing those notes by holding down the string at the fifth fret (and the fourth fret on the G string), we will look at playing a scale.

Playing the scale will be done the same. You will hold down the string on the fret board and pluck it to make a sound. We will start with the lowest scale and that will be the notes: E...F... and G... So now it is time to try that. Just first pluck the low E String and let it sound out. You just played your first note. You need to make sure that you did not hold down the string on any fret, just pluck the string open. **Note:** When we say pluck the string open it means that the string will be plucked without touching it with your finger on the frets, no holding down of the string, just pluck it and play that E string open.

Okay.  It should have sounded like a low E note that rings out for a few seconds and then gets quiet as it goes away.  (The string stops vibrating).  From now on, when you read the words saying to play the string 'open' once again, we know that it is being plucked without holding down the string on the fret.  Sorry about that but it is important to make sure you understand the concept of playing open stings.

Now we are going to pluck the open E, then the F note by holding down the string on the fret as shown in the picture, and then pluck the G note by holding down the string on the thrid fret as shown in the picture. (You should see the guitar nut in the picture, and yes this is an old guitar that I played a lot ☺.  The nut indicates that we start at the first fret.)  Do not go on to the next step until you learn to do these three notes:  E- F- G.

That is important.  First we learn to play E F G.  Once you can do that then it is time to start playing the next notes in the musical scale.

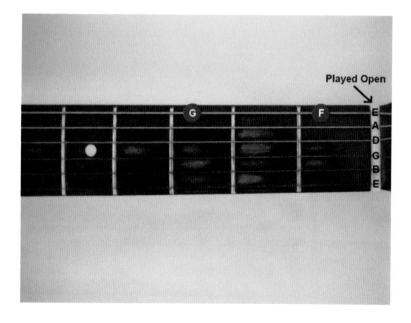

The Musical scale of the guitar starts here in a manner of opinion, but in our training it starts here to learn from. The open E is the first note and then the rest follow like this:

**E F G A B C D E**  This can also be seen as numbers: **1 2 3 4 5 6 7 1**

Notice that the scale always repeats the first note again after it gets to 7. That is to say, every time you reach the seventh note in the scale the next note to follow is note 1 again, not 8.

So that looks like this:  E F G A B C D E, or this:  F G A B C D E F, or this:

A B C D E F G A, and so on.

No matter what note you start on, after you go up the scale and reach the seventh note it starts over to the note you began on. The only difference in the note this time is that it is eight notes higher, but it is still the same note. The first E is still an E note when you come to it eight notes higher, only it is what is known as an octave higher. Someone who can sing with a three octave range, or sing the E note, then sing the E note eight notes higher, then sing the E note eight more notes higher. Wow that is three octaves.

For our lesson we will continue on the major E scale because the guitar is in the key of E.

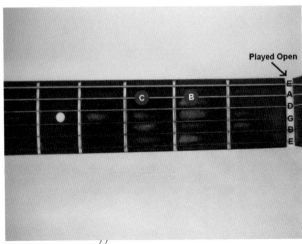

You should now be able to play: Open E, fingered fret F, and fingered fret G. If so it is time to go on to the rest of the scale and learn to play those notes.

Okay now that you can play the first 3 notes; one open, and two fingered, it is time to do the rest. So go ahead and play: E F G, then open A, and then B and C. Of course the red dots are where you put your fingers one red dot at a time. It goes like this: Open E, fingered F, then fingered G, then open A (next string down), then fingered B, and then fingered C. When you play them all together you will get this:

E F G A B C

Each note has a pitch a little higher than the one before it, so that means you are playing notes that go up the scale.

You should be able to play both open and fingered notes now. You should practice if you cannot quite get the fingered notes to sound so good. Don't get discouraged if the note does not come out too well. As long as you are learning what is being shown then you can go on and continue. Before you continue you must learn to play the notes that have been shown so far. Once you are good at playing them you should continue to add more notes up the scale. Ask a family member if you are doing well up to this point. If you are and they say yes, then lets carry on with playing octaves of notes. If they say no, then practice the notes and play them until you get it as described so far in this training.

Don't worry if the scale sounds boring. Once your fingers learn to do this scale, they will develop to be able to play those notes in all kinds of ways that you will make them sound very neat! I am sorry but I have to show you what makes your fingers learn to hold down notes and why these notes have names. You will soon get past this after you practice it. All we guitarists had to drill through this in the beginning. ☺

So here are the rest of the notes covering over three octaves. That means you will reach the note you started on, the open E, three times. They are just octaves higher.

Now that we have learned to play notes both open and fingered up to this point:

E F G A B C, it is now time to pluck the D open and then finger the E (An octave higher) then F.

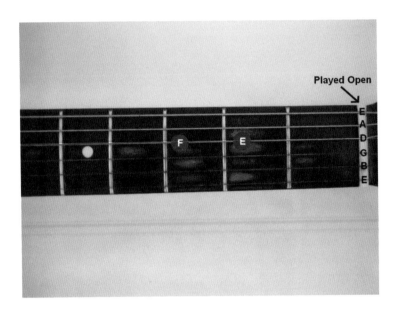

Next is open G, then A. Then open B, after that fingered C, and then fingered D.

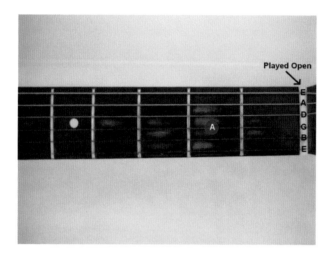

Don't forget the open B to be plucked before the fingered C and D.

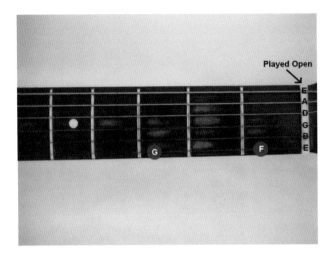

Now the open E (Three octaves higher), then fingered F, and after that fingered G. Now the E-Major scale can be played on and on but let us just learn to do it with just this part of our guitar fret board, close to the headstock. You will certainly do more on the fret board as you get better. Okay, here is the whole thing in the picture below:

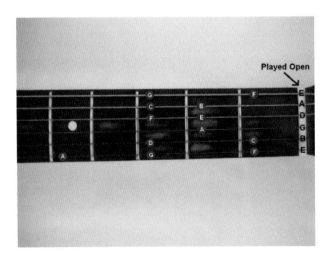

You should now know that you have the open notes shown on the nut, and the red dots are the fingered ones, just keep playing this three octave scale until you can do it kind of fast.  Start at the low E and play all the red dots you see in the pictures.  And even say the notes as you play.  Doesn't have to be said out loud but think the notes as you go…

E F G A B C D E F G A B C D E F G…

One day after mastering the above training you will expand into lead guitar.  After you get good at this scale seek out a book on scales and keep learning them.  I believe that all beginners should learn more than chords. They should learn to play single NOTES!

Also single notes are used in millions of songs as well as learning two-string power chords like in Rock and Country music.  So get those fingers working well on single notes.  But now it is time to get ready to go into learning chords. ☺

# 6 STRUMMING CHORDS

I am pretty sure that you have already learned, and kept in mind the name of each guitar string. And also that you have learned the scale starting out in the key of E when we played up three octaves. If you think you still need to master it, you just have to go back to Chapter 5.

Basically, the frets that are on your guitar neck are there to mark the pitch. If you hold a fret that is closer to the body, you will create a higher pitch. But if you hold a fret closer to the headstock,

then you will create a lower pitch. We know that principle from chapters 4, and 5, right? **Now it is time to learn how to play chords.** The chords are called that because they consist of two or more single notes that will be strummed instead of plucked. When you pluck a single note, you really picked the sting or note, by itself. When you play a chord we will not pick the notes.

Not at first, because first we need to learn how to strum. Before we begin we will look at the scale again. (I know we spent a tremendous amount of time on that already. Don't worry; we just need

to understand one more thing).

When we played the scale in the key of E, we played only major notes. But if we wanted to, we could have plucked the notes half way in between the ones we did pluck. Those ones half way in between are known as sharps and flats. Learning about sharps and flats are beyond this beginners training, but I point it out now because you will understand why we have **Major Chords and Minor Chords.** The Major chord is using two or more notes to form a chord that is a major chord in the scale, or a whole step.

But the Minor chord is using two or more notes to form a chord that is a minor chord in the scale, or a half step. Sharps and Flats are half steps. They are the notes that are in between the ones we learned.

All instruments for the most part have the capability to produce half steps or sharps and flats. It works something like this: If you play the notes E then F that is a whole step in the scale. But if you play the notes E, E sharp, then F you played three notes E then E sharp which is a half step, then F. See how E sharp was only halfway to F? In a Major scale we skip the half notes. Just like on a piano, the little black keys are half steps or sharps and flats. The big white ones are major notes, or whole steps.

Now let's begin the training on playing chords. (Sherw...☺)

# E-Minor

The first chord that we will practice now is the E-minor.  This is very easy and it will not even make you sweat.  For the E-minor, you just have to place your middle finger on the second fret.  You have to place your finger on the area behind the fret.  Take a look at the image below to understand this better:

This line is the second fret.

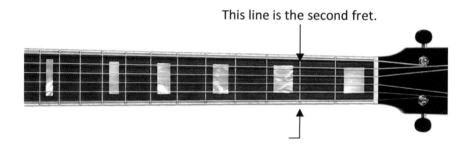

But when we say place your finger on the second fret, you will have to place it here.

So again, place your middle finger on the second fret.  But you have to hold just the A-string.  Hold the string firmly with your finger.  While holding the A-string, place your third finger on second fret too, but on the D-string.  Look at the picture below to see which strings you should be holding.  Notice where the red dots are placed because that is where you should put your fingers.

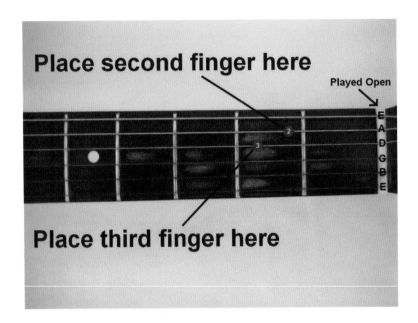

Take a look at this diagram, too.

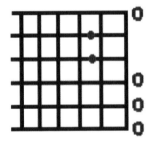

As you can see, there are six horizontal lines here. Those lines are the guitar's strings. There are also six vertical lines in this diagram; those lines are the guitar's frets.

Aside from the lines, you will also see two black dots inside. Now, those dots tell where you should place your fingers. And for this chord, which is the **E-minor**, there is a black dot on the second horizontal line, which means you have to place one finger (your second finger) on the second string from above, which is the A-string.

There is also a dot on the third horizontal line, just below the other dot. That means you have to place another finger (your third finger) on the string below the A-string, which is the D-string. Your first and fourth fingers will not be use in this chord, just keep them away from the strings. Now take a pick or your thumb and fingers of your other hand, and stroke down the strings.

If you were holding down the strings as shown for the E-minor chord then it should sound like the E minor chord. You just strummed a chord. ☺

Take note of this kind of diagram, because this is what we will be using more in this book. You will also notice in the diagram that there are four circles on the right side. Those circles tell you which string you should NOT put your fingers on, at least for this chord only. The circles mean to be strummed open.

So, once you properly place your fingers on the strings based on the diagram, you should strum the strings on the body of your guitar. Just strum (using either your hand or a pick) all the guitar's six strings. Practice the E-minor and strumming for awhile until you get it to sound right and until you are comfortable strumming the chord. (You may need to go back and make sure that your guitar is still in tune!!) **Now let's learn some other chords.**

### G-Major

Of course there are many chords other than the E-minor. So let's go ahead and learn some more chords. This one is the G-Major.

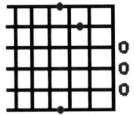

Take a look at this diagram. Unlike in the E-minor chord, there are now three black dots for the G-Major. But what you will do is still somewhat the same. You just have to place your second finger (your middle finger) on the third fret of first string, which is the low E-string (since there is a black dot on the highest horizontal line). And then place another finger (your first finger) on the second fret of the A-string (since there is a black dot on the second horizontal line for the top). Lastly, place another finger (your third finger) on the third fret of the high E-string (since there is a dot on the very bottom horizontal line). Notice also the three circles on the right, which show you where you should not put your fingers on.

After placing your fingers on the correct strings, strum all the strings.
Now you are strumming the G-Major chord. (That's a pretty chord isn't it?)

### C-Major

Another chord is the C-Major. For this chord, take a look at this diagram on the right. As you can see, there are also three black dots for this chord. The things that you have to do are also the same. You just have to place one finger (your third finger) on the third fret of the A string (since there is a black dot on the

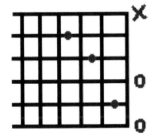

second horizontal line from the top), and then another finger (your middle finger) on the second fret of the D-string (since there is a dot on the third horizontal line, and lastly place a finger (your first finger) on the first fret B-string (since there is a dot on the second from the bottom horizontal line).

You can also see the circles here. Again, you should not put your finger on those parts. But you can also see an X on the right. The X tells you that you should not strum that string. So unlike in the previous chords where you have to strum all six strings, you just have to strum five. Do not strum the topmost string. So that means you will skip touching that string when you strum. The X means to skip touching the strings it marks.

### D-major

Now, let us go to the D-major. In this chord, you just have to place a finger (your first finger) on the G string at the second fret, and then another one (your third finger) on the third fret B string, and lastly another one (your middle finger) on the second fret high E string.

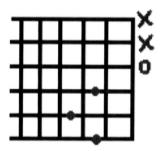

As you will see also, there is a circle and two X's on the right side. This means that while you are holding the chords, you just have to strum four strings. That means with this chord you will skip two, but include the one with the circle as open when strumming the chord. (Four strings only in the strum).

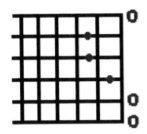

### E-major

Another chord is the E-major. In this one, you only have to do the E-minor chord again to start. The two chords, E-minor and E-major are almost the same, as you can see from the image on the left. But for the E-major chord, you have to add one finger (your first finger) to the first fret of the G-string.

And just like in the E-minor chord, you have to strum all the strings. There is no X in the diagram on this chord. (Mainly because the guitar is in the key of E).

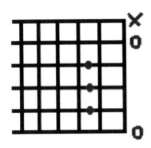

### A-major

For the A-major, you just have to place one finger (your first finger) on the second fret of the D-string, and then another one (your middle finger) on the second fret of the G-string, and then another finger on the second fret B-string.

As you can see on the diagram, the dots are all lined up next to each other. That means your fingers should also be aligned next to each other. But some guitarists prefer to just hold the chord with just one finger. However; like some of the other things we have seen with guitarists, this is not the road to start out on because it is a whole different thing. We should learn to finger the A chord properly at first, using three fingers in line with each other. The 'one finger thing' is a bar chord, and in this training we are not talking about bar chords, but two exceptions are the B and F-chords which use the finger to bar the strings. (Bar chords are advanced training)

Now, strum just five strings, and avoid the one marked by an X.

### A-minor

The last chord for this chapter is the A-minor. For this chord, you have to place a finger (your middle finger) on the second fret/D string, another one (your third finger) on the second fret/G string, and then another one (your first finger) on the first fret/B string.

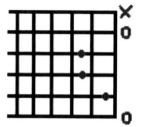

Then you strum only five of the strings. Taking notice where the X and the circles are...X is to be skipped and the circles to be played open. (But you remember that by now. ;)

These seven chords will serve well in our training. Once you know these chords by heart, and if you practice them a lot, then you will be able to master all the other chords as well. That means if you play these chords and make them sound good to the point that they feel natural to you, especially the C-major chord, then your fingers are ready to learn more and more chords that cause you to be able play all kinds of songs.

Both the F-Major and the B-Major chords require bar fingering. So we won't go into those until you can get fluent with the fingering chords shown above. Don't go get a "Guitar Chord Chart" and try and learn all of them yet. It is **extremely important** that you learn the chords shown in this book first. That is very important because you should do like you did when learning to master the scale EFGABCDE up the three octaves. Can you still do that scale...? If you worked it out it should be in your memory now. You would get just as good at these chords by practicing them until you learn them very well.

Then take a chord chart and start by learning the B-Major and the F-Major chords. Remember to take baby steps in order to learn, and then from there you will turn into a great guitarist! ☺

# 7 PLAYING MY FIRST SONG

Shrew!  We have already discussed many things about guitars. We are now down to the last chapter.  Great Job!  I am happy that you made it this far.  This training is designed to have you understanding how to be fluent in playing single notes and playing chords.  But this last chapter is about you playing your very first song on the guitar.

Now, we will practice what you have learned from this book with some exercises.  And then after you have done these exercises, we will proceed to playing your first song on your guitar!  You could skip this if you have already practiced these chords a lot, but if not then just do this first.  Switch between chords and get used to switching in a timing that feels about right for each chord.  Try tapping your foot 4 times as you strum each chord.

**Exercise**

Do these things with your guitar.

1. Stoke up and down four times strumming the E-minor.

2. Stoke up and down four times strumming A-major.

3. Stoke up and down four times strumming E-major.

4. Stoke up and down four times strumming C-major.

5. Stoke up and down four times strumming D-major.

6. Stoke up and down four times strumming G-major.

Can you do this smooth?  If so, here is a song to start out with.

**Playing your first song**

Before you go into playing an entire song, it is important that you first know how to play at least the 7 basic chords.  It is also important that you can properly switch from one chord to another.

By this time, of course, you are still not that ready to easily play songs, especially without making mistakes.  But a little practice will be the best thing for you.  Now, try playing the chorus of Taylor Swift's "You Belong with Me" on your guitar.  The chords are written below:

### You Belong With Me (chorus)

  **D**

If you could see that I'm the one who understands you

   **A**            **Em**

Been here all along, so why can't you see?

      **G**                      **D**

You belong with me, you belong with me.

Those letters—D, A, Em, and G are the chords of the song. D is the D-major chord that we have discussed.  A is the A-major chord, Em is the E-minor chord, and G is the G-major.  Just remember when you are reading chords, that when you see a small letter 'm' it means it is a minor chord.

So now, as to this song, you have to start with the D-major.  As what we have said, when strumming for the D-major, you have to strum only the four bottom strings.  So for the line "If you could see that I'm the one who understands you," you are just playing D-major, since there are no other chords indicated.

When the line "Been here all along, so why can't you see?" comes, you will then shift the chord from D-major to A-major.  Change the chord as you sing the word "Been." And then when the word "You" comes, change the chord from A-major to E-minor.

And when the next line starts and the word "me" comes, you

have to switch chord from E-minor to G-major. And then when the word "with" comes, switch to D-major. Just keep on strumming while you are playing the song. But you have to keep in mind the number of strings you only have to play! This should come with practice naturally.

Did you notice that you have to change chords pretty fast? This is why you had to practice switching from one chord to another. If you can't switch fast enough, then you will not be able to play the song fluently.

When you strum, you need to follow the strumming pattern of the song itself. You will know with time as well as by practicing the song. Try strumming while tapping your foot to keep time. (Time signature is something that is not taught in this book). If you can find simple songs to learn to play you will know the song and the timing will come to you. We tap a foot in order to keep time as we play.

You have to do this again and again until you can play the song fluently. Remember that practice makes things perfect. If it does not sound too great at first that is normal, you have to practice more, an hour or two every day. In the end, you will notice how easy it becomes to play an entire song!

# CONCLUSION

Thank you again for your purchase of this book!

I hope you've enjoyed reading this book on Discovering the Guitar and how to play it. I know that there are tons of books on this to be found, but it was my goal to make it much easier for children who want to learn. That because I had such a hard time understanding the first book I ever learned from. I was frustrated in learning and I couldn't get it right for the longest time. So I wanted to make a book that would help someone learn to play a guitar going by what I believe is the best way to develop. It is a way that will cause the least amount of frustration and the very best way to learn to hold down the guitar strings and make them play.

Finally, if you enjoyed this book, please take the time to share your thoughts and **post a review on Amazon**. It would be greatly appreciated!

Thank you and Good Luck!

Jon P Fox

# A Note About the Author

Author Jon P Fox

Multi-instrumentalist, songwriter, musician, artist and creative director, who spent much of his childhood and early to adulthood, enthused in the making of music and performing. Played in several bands over the years starting in the symphonic band in grade school through Jr. High School where he played the alto saxophone.

After which he took up guitar and went on to form bands of rock genre and wrote many songs that went into production in his make-shift studio. Jon was offered a record contract in 1992 but decided to focus on a new direction in life. He still loves to play his guitar and drums or bass as well as sings and performs his songs both original and covers. Jon is an inspiring author focusing on everything from his talents to commentary on the word of God.

Born and raised in Michigan in 1962, Jon's grandparents migrated from Ireland and his parents were raised in East Detroit. Jon is a professional consultant and aspires in many different hobbies such as Art and Music along with Photography and Video. Jon likes to stay close to God by his attention to the existence of the Holy Spirit, and God's written word!

# Check Out My Other Books

Go ahead and type in the links below to check out the other great books I've published!

Making Time for God   http://www.amazon.com/dp/B00BGI458I
Audio Version:  http://bit.ly/1ht5DTq

Making Time for God Volume 2
http://www.amazon.com/dp/B00F21LXF8

You may also visit my author page here:

https://www.amazon.com/author/jonpfox

Cool Is The Guitar
The Easy to Learn for Kids Guitar Course

Copyright © 2014 Jon P Fox
All Rights Reserved.

Printed in Poland
by Amazon Fulfillment
Poland Sp. z o.o., Wrocław